Do Angels Really Exist?

Dr. Sandra Carter Snyder

DO ANGELS REALLY EXIST?

Unless otherwise indicated, Scripture taken from the HOLY BIBLE, NEW INTERNATIONAL VERSION®. Copyright © 1973, 1978, 1984 by International Bible Society. Used by permission of Zondervan Publishing House. All rights reserved.

Scripture quotations marked KJV are from the King James Version of the Bible.

Author photo: Fabulous Reflections by Julie, www.Fabulousreflectionsbyjulie.com

iUniverse books may be ordered through booksellers or by contacting:

iUniverse
1663 Liberty Drive
Bloomington, IN 47403
www.iuniverse.com
1-800-Authors (1-800-288-4677)

Because of the dynamic nature of the Internet, any web addresses or links contained in this book may have changed since publication and may no longer be valid. The views expressed in this work are solely those of the author and do not necessarily reflect the views of the publisher, and the publisher hereby disclaims any responsibility for them.

Any people depicted in stock imagery provided by Thinkstock are models, and such images are being used for illustrative purposes only. Certain stock imagery © Thinkstock.

ISBN: 978-1-4917-4817-6 (sc)
ISBN: 978-1-4917-4816-9 (e)

Library of Congress Control Number: 2014918527

Printed in the United States of America.

iUniverse rev. date: 11/11/2014

Contents

Acknowledgements

Writing *Do Angels Really Exist?* has brought joy to my life. I know God strategically placed people in my life that helped me prepare this book to share with others. Foremost, I thank My Lord and Savior, Christ Jesus, for the insight to accomplish this task.

- My son, Orlando Ramon Carter, a special acknowledgement and thank you for your support, prayers, and other things too numerous to mention here. God bless you!
- Sanquave Riley, thank you for words of encouragement over the years.
- A heartfelt thanks to you grandson, Deonte' Carter, for your support and patience with my manuscript preparation. Also, to you grandson, Rashad Carter, for making me laugh.
- Dr. Kertis and Dale Hewitt, thank you for your prayers and many words of encouragement in person and via telephone.
- Many thanks to Wayne and Jenny Altman—especially to Jenny who kept asking me, "How's the book coming?"
- Thanks to Erica Browning for always finding time to help me.

- Thanks to my niece, Arnettia, who is smart and intelligent and who always found time to help with my manuscript even during her own busy schedule. I am truly grateful.
- Thanks to my good friend, Daisy Lambert, for your faith and long-time friendship. You always encourage and remind me that there is a hero inside of me—just draw from that inner strength and know everything will be alright.
- Drs. Barbara and Leon Beeler, thank you for your 30 plus years of friendship and mentorship and for always willing to help other people reach their full potential.
- Judith Ponder Brown and Gary Brown, thank you for your humorous and friendly demeanor. Judith, you have been my best girlfriend for over fifty years and I thank you for your true friendship, encouragement, and giving me the word *straight* to help me stay focused and balanced. Love you, girl.
- Thanks to my long time friend, Nikki Ewing, who read the very early draft of this book and continued to believe in me. Thanks for your editorial skills, my friend.
- Thank you, Dr. Evelyn Murray Drayton, for your integrity, wisdom, patience, and assistance. I deeply appreciate the many things you have done to keep this book on track and on time.
- Last, but not least, I thank you, my loving husband, Apostle S. Lee Snyder, for your unwavering support. I truly appreciate you.

Thanks to you, all others not listed, who have prayed for and offered encouragement to me. I offer sincere appreciation to all of you for crossing my path and sharing your love over the years.

Introduction

I have always had an interest in and read about angels in the Bible. Yet, there are many people who question the existence of angels. When people are really nice to us, or when children do cute things that make us laugh, we sometimes call them angels. Yet, I have had experiences with the real spiritual beings we call angels.

As a little girl growing up in Georgia, my parents always reminded me to be nice to strangers because I might be *entertaining angels unaware*. For this reason, I would like to share briefly my personal experience and then move on to share with you information that I believe will persuade you to believe that angels actually are real and they serve us.

I know that I have been protected by angels. Traveling through rain and lightning from South Carolina to Atlanta, Georgia around 4 O'clock one night in 1988, everyone in the car had fallen asleep, including me, the driver. I awaken when I felt the pressing presence of someone else in the vehicle. It felt as if a discerning presence, an angel's wing, had touched my hand on the steering wheel while my car was headed for an embankment. Being fully alert after this touch, I immediately corrected the steering and brought the car back to safety. Through all of this, my husband and son were still asleep and we made a safe trip to Atlanta. I knew the Lord had sent an angel to protect my family and me. As the Scripture says,

"*For he shall give his angels charge over thee, to keep thee in all thy ways*" (Psalm 91:11 KJV).

Enjoy the answers and words of comfort offered in *Do Angels Really Exist?* as it sheds light on the existence and activities of angels. Praise God for His angels.

Chapter One

Angels and Their Creation

The question, *Do angels really exist?* has been at the heart of many studies and discussions over time. At the center of the debate is the reality that angels are beings we cannot see. The *Webster's Collegiate Dictionary* defines an angel as "a spiritual being superior to humans in power and intelligence." We know that angels were God's creation based on Paul's word in Colossians 1:16, where he wrote, *"For by him* [God] *were all things created, that are in heaven, and that are in earth, visible and invisible, whether they be thrones, or dominions, or principalities, or powers."* This verse serves as evidence that angels were God's creation.

Furthermore, Psalm 148:2-5 states: *"Praise ye him, all his angels: praise ye him, all his hosts. Praise ye him, sun and moon; praise him, all ye stars of light. Praise him, ye heavens of heavens. Let them praise the name of the Lord; for he commanded, and they were created."* The part of the Scripture that says, *"For he commanded, and they were created"* lets us know that angels were created by the command that came from the mouth of God.

The following Scripture in Matthew lets us know that Jesus will return to Earth, but only God our Father knows when. However, this same Scripture lets us know that angels are in heaven: "B*ut* *about that day or hour no one knows, not even the angels in heaven, nor the Son, but only the Father"* (Matthew 24:36).

Scriptures tell us angels worship God and that they perform these duties all the time. Satan was jealous over God receiving all of the glory and honor from the angels and allowed pride and resentment to cause his fall from the grace of God. Satan wanted the angels' worship for himself. The prophet Isaiah supports the fact that angels praise and worship God when he spoke in Isaiah 6:2-3:

> *Above it stood the seraphims: each one had six wings; with twain he covered his face, and with twain he covered his feet, and with twain he did fly. And one cried unto another, and said, Holy, holy, holy, is the LORD of hosts: the whole earth is full of his glory.*

In addition, Revelation 4:8-11, similarly talks about angels worshipping God:

> *And the four beasts had each of them six wings about him; and they were full of eyes within: and they rest not day and night, saying, Holy, holy, holy, LORD God Almighty, which was, and is, and is to come. And when those beasts give glory and honour and thanks to him that sat on the throne, who liveth for ever and ever, The four and twenty elders fall down before him that sat on the throne, and worship him that liveth for ever and ever, and cast their crowns before the throne, saying, Thou art worthy, O Lord, to receive glory and honour and power: for thou hast created all things, and for thy pleasure they are and were created.*

The next essential purpose of angels is to carry out the will of God. While God is the creator of heaven and earth, the angels were created to help bridge the gap between God and humans. The Bible contains many references to angels carrying out God's will, especially within the Old Testament where he consistently sent angels to provide instructions to Abraham, Moses, Daniel, and Ezekiel. More specifically, angels rendered a vital role in God's dealing with Israel and their deliverance from Egypt, as well as after they were freed. When the people of Israel refused to follow the word of God delivered by Ezekiel, God sent an angel to mark the people that had been faithful to His word and sent an army of angels to destroy every man, woman and child that did not bear the angel's mark. This serves as evidence that God uses angels to carry out His will (Ezekiel 9:4).

The third essential purpose of angels is to minister God's word to His people. In Hebrews 1:14, angels are described as *"ministering spirits sent to serve those who will inherit salvation."* Furthermore, angels serve at God's command: *"For he shall give his angels charge over thee, to keep thee in all thy ways"* Psalm 91:11 KJV, and from that context, it is God, not man, who commands angels.

God uses angels in several instances throughout the Bible to carry his messages to His people, to carry out His will, and to act as guardians for His people. Angels are referenced in Psalm 68:17 NKJV, as *"the chariots of God"* used in battles against enemies. The Bible addresses angels as seraphim, cherubim, thrones, dominations, virtues, powers, principalities, archangels, and angels and their job is primarily to carry out God's tasks on earth.

In Daniel 12:1 NKJV, Michael is described as the prince of [God's] chosen people based on the Scripture that reads: *"the great prince which standeth for the children of thy people."* The one angel that was prominently mentioned throughout the Bible is Gabriel. He is often referenced in the Bible as the messenger of

3

God (Daniel 8:16, 9:21; Luke 1:19, 1:26). Gabriel is identified as being a messenger concerning the birth of John the Baptist (Luke 1:8-23), as well as the prophesied birth of Jesus Christ to Mary (Luke 1:26-33).

The seraphim and the cherubim are referenced in the Bible in the books of Ezekiel and Isaiah (Ezekiel 1:4-28, 10:3-22; Isaiah 6:2-6). The cherubim are mentioned in Ezekiel as being tied to God's glory (Ezekiel 10). Psalm 80:1 KJV states: *"Thou that dwellest between the cherubim, shine forth."* In Genesis 3:24, the cherubim are referred to the Tree of Life located in Eden.

In Colossians 1:16 KJV, principalities and thrones are described among the ranks of angels created by God. The Scripture reads *"For by him were all things created, that are in heaven, and that are in earth, visible and invisible, whether they be thrones, or dominions, or principalities, or powers: all things were created by him, and for him."* Although principalities are God's creation, various teachings such as Ephesians 6:12, Romans 8:38; 1 Corinthians 15:24; Ephesians 1:21; 3:10; and Colossians 1:16; 2:10, 15 readily associate principalities with evil and negative spirits and forces.

Thrones are referenced in the book of Ezekiel where they appeared before God. Consider the following passage from Ezekiel:

> *And above the firmament that was over their heads was the likeness of a throne, as the appearance of a sapphire stone: and upon the likeness of the throne was the likeness as the appearance of a man above upon it. And I saw as the color of amber, as the appearance of fire round about within it, from the appearance of his loins even upward, and from the appearance of his loins even downward, I saw as it were the appearance of fire, and it had brightness round about. As*

the appearance of the bow that is in the cloud in the day of rain, so was the appearance of the brightness round about. This was the appearance of the likeness of the glory of the LORD (Ezekiel 1:26-28 KJV).

The best descriptions of cherubim that I have read or seen are described in Ezekiel Chapter 10, New International Version (NIV) in its entirety:

I looked, and I saw the likeness of a throne of lapis lazuli above the vault that was over the heads of the cherubim. ² The LORD said to the man clothed in linen, "Go in among the wheels beneath the cherubim. Fill your hands with burning coals from among the cherubim and scatter them over the city." And as I watched, he went in. ³ Now the cherubim were standing on the south side of the temple when the man went in, and a cloud filled the inner court. ⁴ Then the glory of the LORD rose from above the cherubim and moved to the threshold of the temple. The cloud filled the temple, and the court was full of the radiance of the glory of the LORD. ⁵ The sound of the wings of the cherubim could be heard as far away as the outer court, like the voice of God Almighty when he speaks. ⁶ When the LORD commanded the man in linen, "Take fire from among the wheels, from among the cherubim," the man went in and stood beside a wheel. ⁷ Then one of the cherubim reached out his hand to the fire that was among them. He took up some of it and put it into the hands of the man in linen, who took it and went out. ⁸ (Under the wings of the cherubim could be seen what looked like human hands.) ⁹ *I looked, and I saw beside the cherubim four wheels, one beside each of the cherubim; the wheels sparkled like topaz.* ¹⁰ *As for their appearance, the four of them looked alike; each was like a wheel intersecting a wheel.* ¹¹ *As they moved, they would go in any one of the four directions the cherubim faced; the wheels did not turn about as the cherubim went. The cherubim went in whatever direction the head faced, without turning as they went.* ¹² *Their entire bodies, including their backs, their hands and their wings, were completely full of eyes, as were their four wheels.* ¹³ *I heard the wheels being called "the whirling wheels."* ¹⁴ *Each of the cherubim had four faces: One face was that of a cherub, the second the face of a human being, the third the face of a lion, and the fourth the face of an eagle.* ¹⁵ *Then the cherubim rose upward. These were the living creatures I had seen by the Kebar River.* ¹⁶ *When the cherubim moved, the wheels beside them moved; and when the cherubim spread their wings to rise from the ground, the wheels did not leave their side.* ¹⁷ *When the cherubim stood still, they also stood still; and when the cherubim rose, they rose with them, because the spirit of the living creatures was in them.* ¹⁸ *Then the glory of the* Lord *departed from over the threshold of the temple and stopped above the cherubim.* ¹⁹ *While I watched, the cherubim spread their wings and rose from the ground, and as they went, the wheels went with them. They stopped at the entrance of the east gate of the* Lord's *house, and the glory of the God of Israel was above them.* ²⁰ *These were the living creatures I had seen beneath the God of*

Israel by the Kebar River, and I realized that they were cherubim. [21] Each had four faces and four wings, and under their wings was what looked like human hands. [22] Their faces had the same appearance as those I had seen by the Kebar River. Each one went straight ahead.

Now that we have identified some descriptions of angels, we can continue our discussion about the existence of angels. While many people believe that angels exist, some may argue that angels were prevalent only during the Old Testament days. We will find that angels are mentioned in both the Old and the New Testaments.

Chapter Two

Angels in the Old and New Testaments

The Holy Bible references angels from Genesis to Revelation. Some may claim that angels were only mentioned in the Old Testament. Some may claim that angels did not exist during Jesus' walk on this earth. I will show biblical evidence about the existence of angels in the Old and the New Testaments.

The Old Testament

Historical records of angels have existed in the Bible from the very beginning, starting in the book of Genesis. The first reference of an angel takes place in Genesis 3:23-24 where the cherubim are described as guarding the entrance to the Tree of Life. The cherubim were referenced as the angels who stood with flaming swords at the gates of the Garden of Eden. They prevented Adam and Eve from returning to eat the fruit from the Tree of Immortal Life after they were expelled from the Garden. Additionally, stories of encounters with angels are prominent throughout the Bible. Angels appear in the Old Testament to minister and deliver messages from God and are referenced with prominent heroes of the Bible such as Abraham, Jacob, Moses, Ezekiel, and Daniel. During these encounters, the angels acted as messengers of God to warn the people of impending changes, to deliver God's word, and to provide specific directions from God.

Abraham

Abraham, appearing throughout the book of Genesis, has many encounters with angels. He is a significant figure in the Bible because God makes him father of Israel, meaning he is the direct descendent from which we were all created. In the story of Abraham, the initial encounter with an angel involves Hagar, slave to Abraham's wife Sarah. Sarah had given Hagar over to Abraham when she found she [Sarah] was unable to conceive. After Hagar lay with Abraham and became pregnant, Hagar and Sarah argued causing Hagar to flee their home. Her visit from an angel takes place as she is running away from Sarah in Genesis 16. The angel appears before Hagar near a spring in the desert and tells her to return to Sarah. Upon Hagar's return and submission, the angel instructs her to name her unborn baby boy Ishmael. The angel also promises that God will bless Hagar with many descendants.

Later, Scripture details Abraham's encounter with three angels. They inform him that, upon their return the following year, Sarah will bear Abraham a son. Sarah, when she overhears the message, laughs at the thought of bearing a child at such a late stage in her life. Abraham's interaction with the angels is provided in Genesis 18:1-3 KJV:

> *And the LORD appeared to him by the oaks of Mamre, as he sat at the door of his tent in the heat of the day. He lifted up his eyes and looked, and behold, three men stood in front of him. When he saw them, he ran from the tent door to meet them, and bowed himself to the earth, and said, My lord, if I have found favor in your sight, do not pass by your servant.*

It is important to note that the angels appear to Abraham after he has already been told by God in Genesis 17:15 that Sarah will bear him a son and to name him Isaac. As time moved forward, God continued to test Abraham's faith, which leads to another famous biblical story involving Abraham and the sacrificing of his son Isaac. God spoke to Abraham through the voice of an angel in Genesis 22:11, *"And the angel of the Lord called unto him out of heaven, and said, 'Abraham, Abraham' and he said, 'Here am I.'"* The angel instructed Abraham to sacrifice his son Isaac by taking him to the top of a mountain and slit his throat as he would a sacrificial lamb. Isaac's blood would be used as an offering to prove to God that Abraham was prepared to surrender to God's will. In response to the voice, Abraham took Isaac to the top of a mountain, laid him across an altar, and prepared to sacrifice his son. Before he could complete the sacrifice, the angel appeared and commanded him, *"Do not lay a hand on the boy,"* he said. *"Do not do anything to him. Now I know that you fear God, because you have not withheld from me your son, your only son"* (Genesis 22:12). Abraham obeyed and at that moment he caught and sacrificed a ram, offering it up to God in place of his son. Scripture dictates additional communication with Abraham by an angel. Genesis 22:15-18 KJV states:

> *The angel of the LORD called to Abraham from heaven a second time and said, I swear by myself, declares the LORD, that because you have done this and have not withheld your son, your only son, I will surely bless you and make your descendants as numerous as the stars in the sky and as the sand on the seashore. Your descendants will take possession of the cities of their enemies, and through your offspring all nations on earth will be blessed, because you have obeyed me.*

Jacob

Another famous hero in the Bible who encounters angels is Jacob, the grandson of Abraham. He first sees the angels of God in a dream that is described in Genesis 28:12-13, which states: *"He had a dream in which he saw a stairway resting on the earth, with its top reaching to heaven, and the angels of God were ascending and descending on it. There above it stood the LORD."* In the same dream, God promises Jacob that he will inherit his native land and that he and his offspring will be blessed. Jacob awakens from this dream and feels the presence of God. Jacob continues on his way, and while in the land of Laban, he encounters another angel in a dream. The angel tells Jacob to leave and return to his native land. Later, Scripture describes Jacob wrestling with an angel while waiting to cross a stream at the ford Jabbok. The Scripture Genesis 32:24-30 reads:

> *So Jacob was left alone, and a man wrestled with him till daybreak. When the man saw that he could not overpower him, he touched the socket of Jacob's hip so that his hip was wrenched as he wrestled with the man. Then the man said, Let me go, for it is daybreak. But Jacob replied, I will not let you go unless you bless me. The man asked him, What is your name? Jacob, he answered. Then the man said, Your name will no longer be Jacob, but Israel, because you have struggled with God and with humans and have overcome. Jacob said, Please tell me your name. But he replied, Why do you ask my name? Then he blessed him there. So Jacob called the place Peniel, saying, It is because I saw God face to face, and yet my life was spared.*

Jacob, like his grandfather Abraham, experiences many encounters with the angels of God. In his dream where he sees the angels ascending and descending the ladder into heaven, there are no explicit descriptions of the features of the angels. After a wrestling match with an angel, Jacob is renamed Israel. The angel explains the reason for the new name by saying, "B*ecause you have struggled with God and with humans and have overcome*." From that point forward, Jacob was known in the Bible as Israel.

Moses

Moses is yet another one of the famous heroes of the Bible that encountered an angel. The book of Exodus details three separate instances where Moses was spoken to by an angel of God. The first took place when he was called by the angel of the Lord to the burning bush. Exodus 3:1-6 reads:

> *Now Moses was tending the flock of Jethro his father-in-law, the priest of Midian, and he led the flock to the far side of the wilderness and came to Horeb, the mountain of God. There the angel of the LORD appeared to him in flames of fire from within a bush. Moses saw that though the bush was on fire it did not burn up. So Moses thought, I will go over and see this strange sight—why the bush does not burn up. When the LORD saw that he had gone over to look, God called to him from within the bush, Moses! Moses! And Moses said, Here I am. Do not come any closer, God said. Take off your sandals, for the place where you are standing is holy ground. Then he said, I am the God of your father the God of Abraham, the God of Isaac and the God of Jacob. At this, Moses hid his face, because he was afraid to look at God.*

God used His angel to convey the message to Moses that he had been ordained to deliver the Israelites out of Egypt. This Scripture provides further evidence that God used His angels as a channel between heaven and the human realm and to deliver His word.

While God remained with Moses throughout his journey into Egypt, he did not see the angel of the Lord again until after he appeared before Pharaoh to deliver God's message. When Moses and the Israelites came upon the Red Sea, they cried out to the Lord for help. It was at this point that the angel of God revealed himself to Moses and moved from his place of protection in front of the Israelites to take up position behind. Exodus 14:19-20 states the following:

> *Then the angel of God, who had been traveling in front of Israel's army, withdrew and went behind them. The pillar of cloud also moved from in front and stood behind them, coming between the armies of Egypt and Israel. Throughout the night the cloud brought darkness to the one side and light to the other side; so neither went near the other all night long.*

Here, God used an angel to offer protection for the Israelites by hiding them from Pharaoh's army until Moses was able to part the Red Sea and the army of Israel could cross over.

The story of Moses provides insight and confirmation into the role of angels. The encounters with angels referenced throughout the Bible have described angels as messengers carrying forth God's word and as warriors fighting God's battles on Earth. Moses experienced both aspects of these roles. An angel delivered God's message at the burning bush telling Moses to go forth and free the Israelites, and then God provided another angel to go forth and offer protection as the Israelites fled Egypt.

The third reference to Moses interacting with an angel of God took place three months after the Israelites escaped Egypt. Moses was called forth to the top of Mount Sinai where he remained for forty days and forty nights. There at the top of the mountain, God dictated the Ten Commandments to Moses and provided him with a guardian angel to go before him to prepare the lands of Amorites, Hittites, Perizzites, Canaanites, Hivites and Jebusites. Exodus 23:20-23 provided the details of that interaction.

> *See, I am sending an angel ahead of you to guard you along the way and to bring you to the place I have prepared. Pay attention to him and listen to what he says. Do not rebel against him; he will not forgive your rebellion, since my Name is in him. If you listen carefully to what he says and do all that I say, I will be an enemy to your enemies and will oppose those who oppose you. My angel will go ahead of you and bring you into the land of the Amorites, Hittites, Perizzites, Canaanites, Hivites and Jebusites, and I will wipe them out.*

Again, God provided Moses with instructions and then sent a guardian angel to watch over Moses and the Israelites as they carried out God's orders.

Ezekiel

Ezekiel is one of the many prophets in the Bible that had multiple encounters with angels. Ezekiel, who grew up in Jerusalem, was captured and taken to Babylon. His visions and encounters with the angels of God led to him being named the "watchman" for God. In Ezekiel 1:4-28, he described a vision of a cloud of wind that produced four living creatures that were later confirmed in Ezekiel 10:20-22 to be a description of the cherubim.

In the vision, the cherubim were described as looking similar to man but having four faces, four wings, and feet shaped like the sole of a calf. The vision further described the cherubim's wings as joined together and appeared as wheels in the middle of wheels. Ezekiel recognized these creatures as the likeness of God and fell upon his face to worship their presence.

A messenger of God appeared again to Ezekiel several years later and the visit is depicted in Ezekiel 8:1-4:

> *In the sixth year, in the sixth month on the fifth day, while I was sitting in my house and the elders of Judah were sitting before me, the hand of the Sovereign LORD came on me there. I looked, and I saw a figure like that of a man. From what appeared to be his waist down he was like fire, and from there up his appearance was as bright as glowing metal. He stretched out what looked like a hand and took me by the hair of my head. The Spirit lifted me up between earth and heaven and in visions of God he took me to Jerusalem, to the entrance of the north gate of the inner court, where the idol that provokes to jealousy stood. And there before me was the glory of the God of Israel, as in the vision I had seen in the plain.*

While this passage does not specifically refer to the figure of the man as an angel, a conclusion can be drawn that the man represented an angel of God. This is based upon earlier accounts of similar circumstances with Moses and the burning bush. Like Moses, Ezekiel was functioning as a prophet set forth to deliver the words of God to the people of Israel. Further, this Scripture was followed by a description of God on the throne of the cherubim. Ezekiel 9:1-6 reads:

Then I heard him call out in a loud voice, Bring near those who are appointed to execute judgment on the city, each with a weapon in his hand. And I saw six men coming from the direction of the upper gate, which faces north, each with a deadly weapon in his hand. With them was a man clothed in linen who had a writing kit at his side. They came in and stood beside the bronze altar. Now the glory of the God of Israel went up from above the cherubim, where it had been, and moved to the threshold of the temple. Then the LORD called to the man clothed in linen who had the writing kit at his side and said to him, Go throughout the city of Jerusalem and put a mark on the foreheads of those who grieve and lament over all the detestable things that are done in it. As I listened, he said to the others, Follow him through the city and kill, without showing pity or compassion. Slaughter the old men, the young men and women, the mothers and children, but do not touch anyone who has the mark. Begin at my sanctuary. So they began with the old men who were in front of the temple.

Again the Scripture references the man in white linen in conjunction with his description of the God above the cherubim. A conclusion can be made that these references are to angels that God has called forth to carry out His will. The man in white linen was sent through the city to mark people that were against widespread idolization in an effort to ensure they were spared God's wrath. The actions of God using the man in white linen to mark the people of the city show His use of angels to spare and save lives. In addition to the description of the cherubim in the Scripture, this passage also lends evidence of God using angels to destroy. Genesis 19:13 demonstrates the use of angels to destroy based on God's will when they were sent to deliver the message to Lot that they were there to destroy the city.

Daniel

When God sought to provide Daniel with visions of the future, he had many encounters with angels. Even during his youth, Daniel could be described as a man of faith. The story of Daniel in the lion's den has been used as an example of how faith in God's word offers us protection from those that seek to harm us. It is also during this story that we encounter Daniel's first vision of an angel sent by God to help him. In many of his encounters, the angels were used to provide Daniel with understanding of the messages he was being sent by God.

The story of Daniel in the lion's den took place as a result of jealousy from the bureaucrats and administrators of King Darius. They saw the king's pleasure with Daniel's work as a threat to their continued ability to accept bribes and make unjust decisions and laws. To prevent King Darius from making Daniel a prime minister, they had the king sign a law forbidding all his subjugates from praying to any God other than the king. If this law was broken the guilty person was to be thrown into the lion's den. Daniel continued to do as he had always done and prayed three times per day. When the bureaucrats and the administrators learned of his prayer, they turned him in to the king. Daniel was placed in the den of lions but remained unharmed. When the king returned the following morning to see if Daniel was still alive, Daniel replied, *"My God sent His angel and he shut the mouths of the lions. They have not hurt me, because I was found innocent in His sight. Nor have I ever done any wrong before you, Your Majesty"* (Daniel 6:22).

While this Scripture does not offer a description of the angel, nor does it provide specific details of whether Daniel was able to see the angel with his own eyes, it does lend support to the notion that God used His angels as protectors in times of need. Daniel was watched over in the den of the lions and remained untouched based on God's decree that he did nothing wrong. It can be determined that when we are honoring God's word and following His direction, he will offer us protection in the most detrimental circumstances.

Daniel 8:15-19 KJV provides insight into Daniel's interaction with Gabriel on the banks of Ulai. The Scripture reads:

> *And it came to pass, when I, even I Daniel, had seen the vision, and sought for the meaning, then, behold, there stood before me as the appearance of a man. And I heard a man's voice between the banks of Ulai, which called, and said, Gabriel, make this man to understand the vision. So he came near where I stood: and when he came, I was afraid, and fell upon my face: but he said unto me, Understand, O son of man: for at the time of the end shall be the vision. Now as he was speaking with me, I was in a deep sleep on my face toward the ground: but he touched me, and set me upright. And he said, Behold, I will make thee know what shall be in the last end of the indignation: for at the time appointed the end shall be.*

Gabriel appeared again to Daniel in Daniel 9:21-27 while Daniel is praying and confessing the sins of the people of Israel to God. During this encounter, Gabriel was sent to provide Daniel with skill and understanding for dealing with the end of time. The significance of this particular chapter is that Daniel prophesies the coming of the Messiah, as well as the future for Israel. Through his interaction with Gabriel, Daniel was given understanding of the significance of the Messiah, as well as of the events that will lead to his arrival.

Daniel's next encounter with an angel came after he had been praying and fasting for twenty-one days. He was mourning over the plight of Israel and the wars taking place in Jerusalem. While praying and fasting, a messenger explained to Daniel that God had heard his prayers and acknowledged his supplications from the beginning. He explained he [the angel] was held up fighting the kingdom of Persia until Michael, the chief of princes, was sent to offer assistance.

The New Testament

The presence of angels throughout the New Testament is some of the most profound encounters of the Bible. Within the New Testament, angels take part in foretelling the birth of John the Baptist and play a vital role in the birth of Jesus Christ. Angels were forever present around the birth of Christ, throughout His life, and play an important part in His resurrection.

My examination of the New Testament as it relates to angels will include an overview of the life of Zechariah and the role angels played in predicting the birth of John the Baptist. I will also address Gabriel's visit to the Virgin Mary foretelling of the birth of Jesus Christ. A detailed overview of angelic involvement in the life of Christ will follow, and the overview will conclude with a look at Peter the apostle, and angels in the book of Revelation.

Zechariah

Zechariah was a priest that served under King Herod of Judea where he was part of the priestly division Abijah. The priestly divisions took turns rotating duties in the temple worshipping God. One of the highest honors of duties performed at the temple was going into the temple of God and burning incense. During one of his weeks of serving at the temple, Zechariah was given this distinct honor to burn incense in the temple of God. During this particular event, Zechariah encountered a visit from the angel Gabriel for the first time. Gabriel spoke with Zechariah and told him that his wife, Elizabeth, would bear him a son and his name would be John. Gabriel also foretold that John would be important to God and that he would be filled with the Holy Ghost. An overview of this account is provided in Luke 1: 11-17:

Then an angel of the Lord appeared to him, standing at the right side of the altar of incense. When Zechariah saw him, he was startled and was gripped with fear. But the angel said to him: Do not be afraid, Zechariah; your prayer has been heard. Your wife Elizabeth will bear you a son, and you are to call him John. He will be a joy and delight to you, and many will rejoice because of his birth, for he will be great in the sight of the Lord. He is never to take wine or other fermented drink, and he will be filled with the Holy Spirit even before he is born. He will bring back many of the people of Israel to the Lord their God. And he will go on before the Lord, in the spirit and power of Elijah, to turn the hearts of the parents to their children and the disobedient to the wisdom of the righteous—to make ready a people prepared for the Lord.

While Zechariah heard and understood the message given to him by Gabriel, he remained unconvinced because he believed he and Elizabeth were too old to bear children. When Zechariah questioned Gabriel about his ability to trust what he was hearing, Gabriel replied, "*I am Gabriel. I stand in the presence of God, and I have been sent to speak to you and to tell you this good news.*

And now you will be silent and not be able to speak until the day
this happens, because you did not believe my words, which will
come true at their appointed time" (Luke 1:19-20).

Mary and Joseph

Zechariah and his wife Elizabeth play an important role in
preparing the way for the birth of Jesus Christ. Their son, John,
was to be born to preach the gospel of God's word in preparation
for Jesus' ministry. The bloodline of Zechariah and Elizabeth
was indeed blessed by God because Jesus' mother, the Virgin
Mary, was a blood relative to Elizabeth. After Mary was visited
by Gabriel, she went to visit Elizabeth, whereupon Elizabeth
proclaimed Gabriel's foretelling to be true.

The Birth of Jesus Foretold

Angels have contributed towards many events throughout the
Bible, but none of those events were as important and vital to our
history as the foretelling of the birth of Jesus Christ. Gabriel was
the angel chosen by God to visit the Virgin Mary and prepare her
for the coming birth of the Son of God. It is important to note
that Gabriel's visit to Mary came during Elizabeth's sixth month
of pregnancy foreshadowing God's link between the tasks set
forth for John the Baptist and the tasks that would be completed
by Jesus. When Gabriel came to Mary, she was an unmarried
young Jewish girl living in Nazareth, but promised to be married
to Joseph. Upon his visit, Gabriel said unto her:

> *Greetings, you who are highly favored! The Lord*
> *is with you. Mary was greatly troubled at his*
> *words and wondered what kind of greeting this*
> *might be. But the angel said to her, Do not be*
> *afraid, Mary; you have found favor with God.*
> *You will conceive and give birth to a son, and you*

> *are to call him Jesus. He will be great and will be called the Son of the Most High. The Lord God will give him the throne of his father David, and he will reign over Jacob's descendants forever; his kingdom will never end. How will this be, Mary asked the angel, since I am a virgin? The angel answered, The Holy Spirit will come on you, and the power of the Most High will overshadow you. So, the holy one to be born will be called the Son of God. Even Elizabeth your relative is going to have a child in her old age, and she who was said to be unable to conceive is in her sixth month. For no word from God will ever fail. I am the Lord's servant, Mary answered. May your word to me be fulfilled. Then the angel left her* (Luke 1:28-38).

Mary's encounter with Gabriel was the first of many encounters she and Joseph would have during the course of her pregnancy. Joseph, being a newly married man, was skeptical of Mary's fidelity when he learned of her pregnancy. He sought to divorce her quietly so that he could spare her public humiliation. However, before he was able to make arrangements, he was visited by an angel that encouraged him to take Mary as his wife and explained the significance of her pregnancy. Matthew 1:20-21 states "...*an angel of the Lord appeared to him in a dream and said, Joseph, son of David, do not be afraid to take Mary home as your wife, because what is conceived in her is from the Holy Spirit. She will give birth to a son, and you are to give him the name Jesus, because he will save His people from their sins.*"

Here is a clear indication of God using His angels as messengers to deliver His word and to console. God knew Joseph would be shaken by Mary's account that she was impregnated by the Holy Spirit thereby allowing her to remain a virgin. God used His angel to ease Joseph's fears and provide him with the necessary information to keep Mary safe until the Son of God could be born. Even after Joseph made the decision to follow God's direction, he continued to receive visits from angels in his dreams advising him to make decisions that would safeguard Mary and the newborn Jesus against harm.

The Pronouncement of Jesus' Birth

On the night that the Savior was born, there were shepherds tending to their sheep in the field. An angel appeared before them to announce the birth of Jesus. Their encounter with the angel is presented in Luke 1: 9-14 where it states:

> *An angel of the Lord appeared to them, and the glory of the Lord shone around them, and they were terrified. But the angel said to them, Do not be afraid. I bring you good news that will cause great joy for all the people. Today in the town of David a Savior has been born to you; he is the Messiah, the Lord. This will be a sign to you: You will find a baby wrapped in cloths and lying in a manger. Suddenly a great company of the heavenly host appeared with the angel, praising God and saying, Glory to God in the highest heaven, and on earth peace to those on whom His favor rests.*

The shepherds were shocked but went to see if what the angel said was true. When they found Mary and Joseph in Bethlehem, they spread the word of the birth of Christ. Again this verse lends support to the theory that God used His angels as messengers.

Angels of Protection

After accepting that Mary had been chosen to birth the Son

of God, Joseph learned to trust God and follow His direction for keeping Mary and Jesus safe. Shortly after Jesus was born, Joseph was awakened by an angel in a dream warning him of upcoming danger. The angel said, *"...Get up,"* *...take the child and his mother and escape to Egypt. Stay there until I tell you, for Herod is going to search for the child to kill him"* (Matthew. 2:13). King Herod was searching for Jesus and wanted him dead.

Joseph and Mary remained in Egypt until Joseph was again visited by an angel in his dream. The angel said, *"...Get up, take the child and his mother and go to the land of Israel, for those who were trying to take the child's life are dead"* (Matthew. 2:20). Joseph did as the angel asked; thereby, fulfilling the prophecy (Hosea 11:1) that God would call His Son out of Egypt. Joseph and Mary returned to the district of Galilee and remained in the town of Nazareth, where Jesus grew in strength and began teaching God's word.

Crucifixion of Jesus Christ

At the age of thirty, Jesus was baptized by John the Baptist and He received the Holy Ghost. Immediately following His baptism, Jesus was led by God into the wilderness where He stayed in prayer and supplication for forty days and forty nights. During this time, He was tempted by Satan and challenged to defy God's word. At the end of His forty days, God sent His angels to minister to Jesus before He returned to His disciples. This account with angels is described in Matthew 4:11 which states, *"Then the devil left Him, and angels came and attended Him."* The appearance of God's angels to Jesus after Satan leaves is vital because they were sent to attend to His needs.

Jesus remained strong and continued to preach the gospel until it neared the time for His crucifixion. He was again visited by an angel to strengthen Him and prepare Him for His upcoming death on the cross. Jesus Christ knew He was going to be beaten and tortured so, as He entered the Mount of Olives, He prayed earnestly to God: *"Father, if you are willing, take this cup from me; yet not my will, but yours be done"* (Luke 22:42). The Bible says, at this point, an angel from heaven appeared and offered Jesus strength to complete the task set before Him. After the angel came, Jesus prayed earnestly until sweat dropped from His body like blood (Luke 22:44). Shortly after this event, Jesus was beaten, crucified, and buried. His body was placed in a tomb wrapped in linen cloth by Joseph of Arimathea.

Resurrection of Jesus Christ

For centuries, as part of Christian tradition during Passover, the story has been told of how Jesus arose from the dead and ascended into heaven. The part of the story that does not get told very often is the role angels played in His ascension. In addition, there are various accounts of this event, as well as, how Jesus' body was declared missing. Below are descriptions of the event from His disciples, Luke and Matthew.

Three days after Jesus' death, the women went to His tomb and found the stone rolled away. Inside, the body of Jesus Christ was gone, and they were confronted by two men. Luke 24:4-8 reads:

> *While they [the women] were wondering about this, suddenly two men in clothes that gleamed like lightning stood beside them. In their fright, the women bowed down with their faces to the ground, but the men said to them, Why do you look for the living among the dead? He is not here; he has risen! Remember how he told you, while he was still with you in Galilee: The Son of Man must be delivered over to the hands of sinners, be*

> *crucified and on the third day be raised again.*
> *Then they remembered His words.*

While this Scripture does not specifically call the two men angels, they are described as "gleamed like lightning" which suggests that they were angels. On the other hand, Matthew 28:1-10 mentions only one angel but his appearance was like lightning also:

> *After the Sabbath, at dawn on the first day of*
> *the week, Mary Magdalene and the other Mary*
> *went to look at the tomb. There was a violent*
> *earthquake, for an angel of the Lord came down*
> *from heaven and, going to the tomb, rolled back*
> *the stone and sat on it. His appearance was like*
> *lightning, and His clothes were white as snow.*
> *The guards were so afraid of him that they shook*
> *and became like dead men. The angel said to the*
> *women, Do not be afraid, for I know that you*
> *are looking for Jesus, who was crucified. He is*
> *not here; he has risen, just as he said. Come and*
> *see the place where he lay. Then go quickly and*
> *tell his disciples: He has risen from the dead and*
> *is going ahead of you into Galilee. There you*
> *will see him. Now I have told you. So the women*
> *hurried away from the tomb, afraid yet filled with*
> *joy, and ran to tell his disciples. Suddenly Jesus*
> *met them. Greetings, he said. They came to him,*
> *clasped his feet and worshiped him. Then Jesus*
> *said to them, "Do not be afraid. Go and tell my*
> *brothers to go to Galilee; there they will see me.*

Peter the Apostle

It appears that the apostle Peter was one of Jesus' most trusted disciples. He was loyal to Jesus and trusted Him beyond measure. He remained that way during his time with Christ, until the time came for Jesus to be crucified. Even as Jesus told Peter that he would deny Him, Peter argued that he would never perform such an act of deceit. After Jesus died and arose from the dead, it was Peter that He sought out among His disciples. After Jesus ascended into Heaven, Peter defected first from the Jewish sect and became the first apostle to preach on the day of Pentecost. For the next fifteen years, Peter continued to preach the word of the New Covenant until he came to the Mediterranean city of Caesarea. At Caesarea, he introduced the Gentiles to the Christian faith, which resulted in his imprisonment.

On the night before Peter was to be brought to trial, God sent an angel to release Peter. In his cell, Peter was bound with two chains and the entrance to his cell was guarded by sentries. An account of what happened next is provided in Acts 12:7-11:

> *Suddenly an angel of the Lord appeared and a light shone in the cell. He struck Peter on the side and woke him up. Quick, get up! he said, and the chains fell off Peter's wrists. Then the angel said to him, Put on your clothes and sandals. And Peter did so. Wrap your cloak around you and follow me, the angel told him. Peter followed him out of the prison but he had no idea that what the angel was doing was really happening; he thought he was seeing a vision. They passed the first and second guards and came to the iron gate leading to the city. It opened for them by itself and they went through it. When they had walked the length of one street, suddenly the angel left him.*

> *Then Peter came to himself and said, Now I know*
> *without a doubt that the Lord has sent his angel*
> *and rescued me from Herod's clutches and from*
> *everything the Jewish people were hoping would*
> *happen.*

The story of apostle Peter reiterates the magnitude of God's power. God sent an angel into Peter's prison cell to release and strategically direct him without being seen or heard by his guards. Even after it was discovered Peter was gone, the guards had no recollection of what happened and King Herod was unable to locate Peter. The angel in this story not only came to offer protection for Peter in his time of trouble, he was also used to remove Peter from the cell.

Angels in the Book of Revelation

Angels have been repeatedly shown to be the messengers of God, protectors of His people and the earth, and to carry out His will. As we move to the end of the Bible, angels play an important role in the end of days. The book of Revelation is a foreshadowing of God's destruction of the world; a time when angels will again walk the earth with man. In Revelation, the role of angels in the end of days is described. Angels will be shown to grace the throne of God and offer worship; they will unleash the Apocalypse; they will sound the trumpets; and unleash seven plagues upon the earth.

John the Apostle

The book of Revelation begins with Jesus sending an angel to His servant John the apostle, to provide him with the events that will take place in the end of days. Revelation 1:1 says, *"He [Jesus] made it known by sending His angel to His servant John, who testifies to everything he saw – that is, the word of God and the testimony of Jesus Christ.*" This Scripture provides insight in the shift in hierarchy for angels. Before Jesus' ascension, angels took their direction from God. By way of this Scripture, Jesus now has the authority to command the angels to do God's work. Revelation 4:2-8 describes the vision of angels within heaven that John the apostle saw:

> *At once I was in the Spirit, and there before me was a throne in heaven with someone sitting on it. And the one who sat there had the appearance of jasper and ruby. A rainbow that shone like an emerald encircled the throne. Surrounding the throne were twenty-four other thrones, and seated on them were twenty-four elders. They were dressed in white and had crowns of gold on their heads. From the throne came flashes of lightning, rumblings and peals of thunder. In front of the throne, seven lamps were blazing. These are the seven spirits of God. Also in front of the throne there was what looked like a sea of glass, clear as crystal. In the center, around the throne, were four living creatures, and they were covered with eyes, in front and in back. The first living creature was like a lion, the second was like an ox, the third had a face like a man, the fourth was like a flying eagle. Each of the four living creatures had six wings and was covered with eyes all around, even under its wings.*

Here, John the apostle describes angels that stand before God in heaven and constantly worship God. Consider this portion of Revelation 4:8, "*Day and night they never stop saying: 'Holy, holy, holy is the Lord God Almighty, who was, and is, and is to come.*'"

Angels and the Tribulation of Judgment

Angels appear again in Chapter 5 of Revelation, as John the apostle continues the vision he started in Chapter 4. At this point, God reveals the truth behind the scroll containing seven messages or the Tribulation judgments of God. Each message contained within the scroll had been sealed by God. To reveal the message of the scroll, each of the seals must be broken. In John the apostle's vision, an angel called out, *"Who is worthy to break the seals and open the scroll?"* (Revelation 5:2), but he received no reply. Not only that, John the apostle is given a glimpse of the multitude of angels that exist in heaven. In Revelation 5:11-12, the Scripture reads, *"Then I looked and heard the voice of many angels, numbering thousands upon thousands, and ten thousand times ten thousand. They encircled the throne and the living creatures and the elders."* The depiction of angels in Revelation supports the vision seen by Daniel (Daniel 7:10), where he described the angels tending to God's throne. These Scriptures lend evidence to the notion that there are more angels than can be physically counted and their numbers may be infinite.

During the period of Tribulation, an angel of God is sent to mark 144,000 from the twelve different tribes of Israel. Revelation 7:1 describes John the apostle's vision of what takes place after the 144,000 have been marked and before the Tribulation judgment begins. The Scripture reads:

> *After this I saw four angels standing at the four corners of the earth, holding back the four winds of the earth to prevent any wind from blowing on the land or on the sea or on any tree. Then I saw another angel coming up from the east, having the seal of the living God. He called out in a loud voice to the four angels who had been given power to harm the land and the sea: Do not*

harm the land or the sea or the trees until we put
a seal on the foreheads of the servants of our God
(Revelation 7:1-3).

The angels in these Scriptures are performing two important tasks; offering protection from the Tribulation of God, and placing a seal of protection on the foreheads of those that are to remain untouched.

The Seven Seals, the Golden Censer, and the Trumpets

When the seventh seal of the scroll was opened in Revelation 8, the seven angels that always stood before God were given trumpets. Another angel carried the golden censer and stood before the altar of God in preparation for the events to come. The Scripture tells us that the prayers of man were sent up to God through the hand of an angel (Revelation 8:4). The angel filled the censer with fire from the altar of God and threw it down to the earth. Revelation 8:6-13 describes what will happen next:

Then the seven angels who had the seven trumpets
prepared to sound them. The first angel sounded
his trumpet, and there came hail and fire mixed
with blood, and it was hurled down on the earth.
A third of the earth was burned up, a third of the
trees were burned up, and all the green grass
was burned up. The second angel sounded his
trumpet, and something like a huge mountain, all
ablaze, was thrown into the sea. A third of the sea
turned into blood, a third of the living creatures
in the sea died, and a third of the ships were
destroyed. The third angel sounded his trumpet,
and a great star, blazing like a torch, fell from

> *the sky on a third of the rivers and on the springs*
> *of water— the name of the star is Wormwood. A*
> *third of the waters turned bitter, and many people*
> *died from the waters that had become bitter. The*
> *fourth angel sounded his trumpet, and a third of*
> *the sun was struck, a third of the moon, and a*
> *third of the stars, so that a third of them turned*
> *dark. A third of the day was without light, and*
> *also a third of the night. As I watched, I heard an*
> *eagle that was flying in midair call out in a loud*
> *voice: "Woe! Woe! Woe to the inhabitants of the*
> *earth, because of the trumpet blasts about to be*
> *sounded by the other three angels!"*

Revelation 8 offers us insight into two aspects of the work of angels. The first aspect is that our prayers are not to be made to angels, but rather to God. The angel that holds the golden censer merely acts as a transporter whose primary responsibility is to bring our prayers up before God.

The second aspect of angels revealed in these Scriptures is that angels are used to prepare us in times of trouble and despair. The seven angels will be given trumpets, upon which they will sound the alarm to warn us of the coming destruction. Not only do angels sound the trumpets to warn us, the Scripture also describes an eagle, which can be thought of as an angel, flying through the sky warning us further that the last three trumpets will bring about severe destruction.

Chapter 9 of Revelation describes the use of angels sounding the fifth and sixth trumpets during the end days. The fifth trumpet is significant in terms of understanding Satan's descent from heaven. For now, I will focus on the significance of the breaking of the sixth seal. With the sixth trumpet, another wave of God's angels will be released upon the earth. Revelation 9:13-21 reads:

*The sixth angel sounded his trumpet, and I heard
a voice coming from the four horns of the golden
altar that is before God. It said to the sixth angel
who had the trumpet, 'Release the four angels who
are bound at the great river Euphrates.' And the
four angels who had been kept ready for this very
hour and day and month and year were released
to kill a third of mankind. The number of the
mounted troops was twice ten thousand times ten
thousand. I heard their number. The horses and
riders I saw in my vision looked like this: Their
breastplates were fiery red, dark blue, and yellow
as sulfur. The heads of the horses resembled the
heads of lions, and out of their mouths came fire,
smoke and sulfur. A third of mankind was killed
by the three plagues of fire, smoke and sulfur that
came out of their mouths. The power of the horses
was in their mouths and in their tails; for their
tails were like snakes, having heads with which
they inflict injury.*

This Scripture tells us that God released His angels to destroy a third of the world. The people they were sent to destroy are those that have been unrepentant and continue to mock the word of God. The angels are described in detail and offer us understanding that only God can unleash the angels on mankind. They are ever faithful to his command and only act when he grants them authority.

When the seventh trumpet was sounded, the angels of God pronounced, "The *kingdom of the world has become the kingdom of our Lord and of His Messiah, and He will reign forever and ever*" (Revelation 11:15). John the apostle reveals that after the last trumpet has sounded, the seven angels will prepare to deliver the last seven plagues on man. He describes the seven angels in the following passage:

> *Out of the temple came the seven angels with the seven plagues. They were dressed in clean, shining linen and wore golden sashes around their chests. Then one of the four living creatures gave to the seven angels seven golden bowls filled with the wrath of God, who lives forever and ever. And the temple was filled with smoke from the glory of God and from His power, and no one could enter the temple until the seven plagues of the seven angels were completed* (Revelation 15:6-8).

Each of the seven angels pours out the seven plagues one by one, unleashing the wrath of God unto the world.

The Angel and the Little Scroll

In Revelation Chapter 10, John the apostle encounters a similar event as Ezekiel did with a vision of an angel carrying a scroll. John the apostle sees the angel descending from heaven; and as he attempts to record the view, he is told to refrain and listen to the angel. The angel approaches him and instructs him to eat the scroll so that he could go forth and prophesy the word of God. John the apostle's description of the angel encompasses the following:

> *I saw another mighty angel coming down from heaven. He was robed in a cloud, with a rainbow above his head; his face was like the sun, and his legs were like fiery pillars. He was holding a little scroll, which lay open in his hand. He planted his right foot on the sea and his left foot on the land,*

and he gave a loud shout like the roar of a lion"
(Revelation 10:1-3).

In the end, the angel said unto the John the apostle,

> *Do not seal up the words of the prophecy of this scroll, because the time is near." Let the one who does wrong continue to do wrong; let the vile person continue to be vile; let the one who does right continue to do right; and let the holy person continue to be holy"* (Revelation 22:10-11).

The angel's purpose was realized when he ensured God's tasks that John the apostle would carry the prophecy of the end of days to God's people.

Chapter Three

Fallen Angels and Guardian Angels

The descriptions and the roles of angels have been studied among different cultures and religions. With differing narratives, the view of angels and their specific role in religious history is very much dependent upon the type of religion and the religious followers that recorded the history.

Christians believe that angels are spiritual beings created by God before the earth's creation. The role of angels in the Christian faith is to glorify God, bring forth His word and direction, protect God's people, and carry out His chastisement when His word has been forsaken.

Based on the descriptions in the Bible and countless reports initiated by theologians, we know that Satan was once an angel of God and that he defied God's will. We also know that he was the first initiator of sin, and when he chose sin, he taught his ways of deceit to other angels. Consequently, a third of the angels in heaven were cast out along with Satan. Satan and his fallen angels continue to unleash destruction and turmoil even today.

When thinking about how to describe the fallen angels, a few Scriptures from the Bible must be considered. Some of these Scriptures depict past events and some foreshadow events that must yet take place. The first Scripture reference is Isaiah 14:12 where we learn that Satan, also called the *morning star*, was once an angel in heaven. The Scripture reads, *"How you have fallen from heaven, morning star, son of the dawn! You have been cast down to the earth, you who once laid low the nations!"* From this verse, we learn that Satan thought he could lead a rebellion against God without being punished; but, he was cast out for his actions.

In the book of Jude, we discover how God deals with angels that defy His will. Jude 1:6 states, *"And the angels who did not keep their positions of authority but abandoned their proper dwelling—these he has kept in darkness, bound with everlasting chains for judgment on the great Day."* Isaiah 14 provides us with an account of Satan that took place in the past, while Jude 1:6 helps us to understand how Satan and the fallen angels will be dealt with until Judgment Day comes. Another set of Scriptures in the Bible that helps us to identify Satan as a fallen angel is Ezekiel 28:13-19. These verses provide us with a detailed account of why Satan fell. It reads:

> *You were in Eden, the garden of God; every precious stone adorned you: carnelian, chrysolite and emerald, topaz, onyx and jasper, lapis lazuli, turquoise and beryl. Your settings and mountings were made of gold; on the day you were created they were prepared. You were anointed as a guardian cherub, for so I ordained you. You were on the holy mount of God; you walked among the fiery stones. You were blameless in your ways from the day you were created till wickedness was found in you. Through your widespread trade you were filled with violence, and you sinned. So I drove you in disgrace from the mount of God, and I expelled you, guardian cherub, from among the fiery stones. Your heart became proud on account of your beauty, and you corrupted your wisdom because of your splendor. So I threw*

you to the earth; I made a spectacle of you before kings. By your many sins and dishonest trade you have desecrated your sanctuaries. So I made a fire come out from you, and it consumed you, and I reduced you to ashes on the ground in the sight of all who were watching. All the nations who knew you are appalled at you; you have come to a horrible end and will be no more.

Some scholars probably are still arguing whether these actual Scriptures in the Bible are referring to Satan or to some other being. The book of Genesis gives us our first look at Satan and how he comes upon his status as a fallen angel when he tempted Eve to partake of the forbidden fruit. Satan appeared to Eve in the form of a serpent and convinced her that if she ate from the forbidden tree, her eyes "[would] be opened, and [she would] be like God, knowing good and evil" (Genesis 3:5). When God saw this deceit, He cursed the serpent to spend the rest of his days crawling on the ground.

Revelation 12:9 states, *"The great dragon was hurled down—that ancient serpent called the devil, or Satan, who leads the whole world astray. He was hurled to the earth, and his angels with him."* This Scripture specifically calls the serpent the devil and Satan, lending further support that Satan is associated with the serpent snake. Satan is again referenced as a serpent in Revelation 20:2-3 that reads,

He seized the dragon, that ancient serpent, who is the devil, or Satan, and bound him for a thousand years. He threw him into the Abyss, and locked and sealed it over him, to keep him from deceiving the nations anymore until the thousand years were ended. After that, he must be set free for a short time.

This later description references a foreshadowing of how Satan will be dealt with during and after the Tribulation of Judgment.

When Satan is punished, fallen angels will also be punished. It is understood by many that a third of the angels of heaven were cast down with Satan when he fell. To ascertain from Scripture how many angels fell with Satan, it is imperative to consider the origin of name and references to Satan. Throughout the Bible, Satan has been referenced as Lucifer, the morning star, prince of the devil, wicked one, serpent, angel of the bottomless pit, and the great red dragon. When Revelation 12:3-4 refers to the great *red dragon,* it can be concluded that reference is Satan. The Scripture reads: *"Then another sign appeared in heaven: an enormous red dragon with seven heads and ten horns and seven crowns on its heads. Its tail swept a third of the stars out of the sky and flung them to the earth."* In Job 38:7, angels are referred to as *morning stars.* This allows us to make the biblical assumption that Satan's influence had reached a third of the angelic beings in heaven causing them to fall as he fell.

Everyone, in my opinion wants to be able to walk and talk with their own personal angel. We refer to personal angels as our guardian angels and yearn for their divine protection and intervention in our lives. In the book of Daniel, an angel showed up and offered protection for Daniel, a single individual, when Daniel was in the lion's den. When asked how he survived, Daniel replied: "My God sent His angel, and he shut the mouths of the lions" (Daniel 6:22). A single angel was sent by God to protect Daniel in his time of need. Whether or not the angel was present *before* Daniel arrived is irrelevant; the fact is the angel was there at the right time.

Another very interesting story of a guardian angel's intervention is that of Peter's deliverance from prison, found in Acts 12:6-16:

The night before Herod was to bring him to trial, Peter was sleeping between two soldiers, bound with two chains, and sentries stood guard at the entrance. 7 Suddenly an angel of the Lord appeared and a light shone in the cell. He struck Peter on the side and woke him up. "Quick, get up!" he said, and the chains fell off Peter's wrists.8 Then the angel said to him, "Put on your clothes and sandals." And Peter did so. "Wrap your cloak around you and follow me," the angel told him. 9 Peter followed him out of the prison, but he had no idea that what the angel was doing was really happening; he thought he was seeing a vision. 10 They passed the first and second guards and came to the iron gate leading to the city. It opened for them by itself, and they went through it. When they had walked the length of one street, suddenly the angel left him.11 Then Peter came to himself and said, "Now I know without a doubt that the Lord has sent his angel and rescued me from Herod's clutches and from everything the Jewish people were hoping would happen."12 When this had dawned on him, he went to the house of Mary the mother of John, also called Mark, where many people had gathered and were praying. 13 Peter knocked at the outer entrance, and a servant named Rhoda came to answer the door. 14 When she recognized Peter's voice, she was so overjoyed she ran back without opening it and exclaimed, "Peter is at the door!"15 "You're out of your mind," they told her. When she kept insisting that it was so, they said, "It must be his angel."16 But Peter kept on knocking, and when they opened the door and saw him, they were astonished. 17 Peter motioned with his hand for them to be quiet and described how the Lord had brought him out of prison. "Tell James and the other brothers and sisters about this," he said, and then he left for another place.

We can readily see from Scriptures that angels were on assignment to help Peter. Peter concluded that *the Lord* had sent an angel to his rescue. Likewise, angels are available to minister to us in today's society.

Chapter Four

Angelic Encounters In Today's Society

First of all, I do *not* encourage the worship of angels. We are to worship God, not angels. I am not suggesting that anyone pray to angels. You pray to God, in Jesus' name and He knows when to dispatch His angels for duty. I have never ascended to heaven and visited the angels. However, I know angels have descended and visited me. They probably did not come on their own accord, but on the command given by God for an angel to come to my rescue. Similarly, you know whether or not you have experienced invisible support. It may seem to you as if you felt someone else beside you during a dire situation. Don't allow other people to persuade you to doubt that you have had this experience or have met an angel. Maybe you have already entertained angels unaware (Hebrews 13:2).

As stated earlier, Christians believe that angels are spiritual beings created by God before the earth's creation. According to Isaiah 14:12, Satan was once an angel in heaven. After Satan's fall from heaven, along with about one third of the angels in heaven, they have been causing havoc for God's children on earth. Those angels that fell with Satan are referred to as messengers just as God's angels are called messengers:

And lest I should be exalted above measure through the abundance of the revelations, there was given to me a thorn in the flesh, the messenger of Satan to buffet me, lest I should be exalted above measure (2 Corinthians 12:7-9).

And no marvel; for Satan himself is transformed into an angel of light (2 Corinthians 11:14 KJV).

Do you think angelic beings ceased to exist? Although Satan has his messengers, God has faithfully provided for His children using His angelic force. You are being protected by God's messengers just as there were biblical angelic encounters. Since we are spiritual beings, it seems we should be more familiar with heavenly occurrences than the earthly affairs. We probably don't hear about many angelic episodes because some people are reluctant to share their encounters.

People in these modern days have had close calls with tragedies, and even fatalities. At times, it seems people are ashamed or even afraid to discuss bizarre spiritual interventions. But, in reality, I believe we need to be well acquainted with the supernatural world. No one has to fabricate an event to share the reality of angelic existence because there are enough people who are bold enough to share their unique experiences. As a result, hundreds of books and articles are published each year with stories from people that have had near death experiences or other crises.

When the television show, *Touched By An Angel* aired, I was impressed that I could so closely relate to some of the episodes. Many are now claiming to have been visited by angels of God. I have a few stories about angelic encounters that I would like to share as well. I will address a few of my personal angelic encounters in this chapter. In addition, I am honored to share a few angelic interventions by my husband, Apostle S. Lee Snyder, and by one of my dear friends and sister in Christ, Evelyn Murray Drayton.

The Unknown Animal Foot Tracks

We lived in a large forest area where all kinds of animals freely roamed. Residents also liked to fish in the area surrounding our home. As a little girl around seven years old, my siblings and I were outside playing in the hot July sunshine. While we were all having fun, my older sister Joan felt the presence of an unseen guest. For some reason, I also felt the presence. Suddenly, an unfamiliar voice announced that we were to get the smaller children and take them inside the house. Joan and I both even felt a gentle force leading us into the house. We didn't know why we felt this presence ushering us inside the house; but we all gathered inside, got comfortable, and rapidly fell asleep. I don't recall being sleepy, but Joan and I woke up about the same time. There was a strange feeling in the atmosphere, but since the sun was still shining, we all went back outside to play. After just a little while outside, we noticed footprints of a huge animal in the sand. We had heard rumors about panthers or bobcats being in the area and it seemed the footprints belonged to one of those animals.

The strangest thing about all of this is the fact that we had all kinds of domesticated dogs and cats at our house. Yet, during the time we were running inside the house, sleeping, and going back outside, we did not hear even one bark from our dogs. Did the dogs see the animal that made the footprints? If so, why didn't the dogs bark? As years went by, we realized that it had to have been an angel sent by God to usher us in the house and protect us from danger. I believe it was divine intervention that the dogs did not bark to awaken us and cause panic and euphoria among us. Praise God for angels assigned to protect us.

Saved By Angels

I recall one Friday night my husband and I had been invited to a church service. We accepted the invitation and got dressed for the meeting. When we got in the car and drove off, the car performed in a sluggish manner as if it would shut off. We had never had problems with the car before this night. The problem escalated as we traveled and all of a sudden the car stopped. We decided to go back home if the car ever cranked. My husband was able to restart the vehicle and we turned around and went back home. The next day we asked about the meeting. We were anxiously awaiting some good news about the move of God in the service. Instead, we were told to be glad that we did not attend the service because a mass confusion at the facility required Law Enforcement intervention. We concluded that God did not want us to be a part of the uproar; and therefore, angels were assigned to temporarily disable our vehicle. Amazingly, we never had another problem with the vehicle after that scheduled church service.

Protective Glass Shield

I served as a medical assistant to a group of doctors in Atlanta, Georgia. One of my duties was to call patients from the waiting room to perform their initial assessments. My work day also included being a phlebotomist. One day as I was calling a patient, a clear glass square encircled me. I stuck out my hands to feel the glass, but nothing happened. Then I stuck out one of my legs just to see if the glass was really there. I didn't feel any differently and no matter which direction I turned, the glass square remained. The glass square enabled me to discern the different kinds of spirits associated with each patient's personality. This glass square lingered until the end of my work shift. I refer to this clear glass square as my protective shield sent by the Lord to help me deal with some special patients that day.

Avoidable Collision

Late one night as I was traveling from an event in Atlanta, Georgia, a car from the opposite lane was headed directly into my vehicle. I don't know what happened, but in a blink of an eye I felt a quick jerk. The jerk caused me to miss the other vehicle and my life was spared. I know the angel of the Lord protected us from a terrible accident and saved my life, and the life of the other driver. Praise God.

Dogs Be Ware

I visited one of my friends, but I was not aware that her dogs were unrestrained this day. As I exited my car, the two dogs charged and appeared to be ready for an attack. As the huge dogs approached me, I didn't know what to do. A voice told me to be calm, don't be afraid, and stand still. The two huge dogs only circled around me and became calm. I then walked peaceably to my vehicle and returned home unharmed.

Angel To The Rescue

I was traveling out of town at a time I did not have GPS or OnStar services. I was lost! Consequently, I stopped and asked a man for directions. As I turned to thank the man, it seems he had disappeared right before my eyes. I shook my head and blinked my eyes a few times to make sure I was not hallucinating. I recall driving away and telling myself that *it must have been an angel.*

"Let brotherly love continue. Be not forgetful to entertain strangers; for thereby some have entertained angels unawares" (Hebrews 13:2 KJV).

Music In The Air

I had just returned home from visiting my family in Atlanta,

Georgia. I felt very exhausted and decided to tilt my head back and get some well-deserved rest. Suddenly, I heard music resounding in the air. The music brought peace and tranquility that renewed my body, mind, and soul. Later, I opened my eyes and tried to find the music source that brought so much joy to my life, but immediately the music stopped. I don't have words to describe the caliber of music I heard, but it was glorious—it had to be music from heaven. I never heard such a melodious sound again. Praise God.

Traveling Mercies

One late night in 1988, traveling through rain and lightning from South Carolina to Atlanta, Georgia, everyone in the car had fallen asleep, including me, the driver. An angel's wing touched me to awaken me and my hand immediately gripped the steering wheel to avoid hitting an embankment. Being fully alert after this touch, I immediately corrected the steering and brought the car back to safety. Through all of this, my husband and son were still asleep as we arrived safely to Atlanta. I knew the Lord had sent an angel to protect my family and me. I purposely reiterated this incident because, without a doubt, an angel was in my vehicle. My entire household could have been killed simultaneously and I just wanted to express my thanksgiving to God *one more time*.

Beware of Strangers

While in the marketplace one day, a rugged-looking stranger approached me. The man appeared to be nice and sincere as he asked me for some money. His angelic countenance pricked my heart and I gave him the amount he requested. I thought *this could be an angel*. I tried to locate the man to see which direction he turned, but it seemed the man just vanished. I thought to myself again, *it must have been an angel*.

"*Let brotherly love continue. Be not forgetful to entertain strangers; for thereby some have entertained angels unawares*" (Hebrews 13:2 KJV).

The following angelic encounters were shared with me years ago by Apostle S. Lee Snyder (my husband):

Demonic Forces

Years ago, my husband and I evangelized in various cities in the United States to preach the gospel. It seems we were demonically attacked by warlocks and through witchcraft only because we preached the good news. You could almost feel the forces of evil wherever we went. I recall vividly as my husband and I sat in our house one night, we saw angels had surrounded the walls of our home. The Holy Spirit said to my husband, "*The angels are there for your protection and if they were not here, you would not be able to live in this house.*" Angels rescued my husband and me out of the hands of the enemy.

> *When the servant of the man of God got up and went out early the next morning, an army with horses and chariots had surrounded the city. "Oh no, my lord! What shall we do?" the servant asked. "Don't be afraid," the prophet answered. "Those who are with us are more than those who are with them." And Elisha prayed, "Open his eyes, LORD, so that he may see." Then the LORD opened the servant's eyes, and he looked and saw the hills full of horses and chariots of fire all around Elisha* (2 Kings 6:15-17).

Deliverance From An Auto Accident

About 4 p.m. one hot summer day in 1984 while working for Dekalb County Drainage Department, my husband was just a breath away from an auto collision. Two cars had stopped abruptly in front of his truck, causing havoc on the highway, as he tried to avoid the two vehicles. My husband maneuvered the steering as best he could while his truck swerved repeatedly. All of a sudden, he felt the presence of an unseen force controlling the steering wheel, barely escaping an anticipated overturn. The truck was brought to safety and landed near the two stopped vehicles without any fatalities, injuries, or damages to either vehicle.

My husband's boss was behind him in another vehicle and saw the entire incident. His boss said, "All I saw was smoke!" He thought my husband was killed in that accident. However, the boss was grateful to see that all drivers and passengers were able to walk away without a scratch. When my husband drove back to his job and parked, an angel told my husband that he had saved his life. My husband became numb and could not walk for a short period of time. Later, he began to praise God right there in the parking lot. Thank the Lord for angels that protected all those involved in that turmoil.

"Praise him, all his angels; praise him, all his heavenly hosts" (Psalm 148:2).

Airplane Crash Warning

While in church one Friday night, my husband was praying for a friend of the family who was scheduled to visit her relatives out of state. During the prayer, my husband heard the angel of the Lord telling him to inform our friend to cancel her flight. My husband recalled how strangely the woman looked at him as he shared the message. She was startled, but my husband already knew the outcome and hoped she would obey. We were informed later that the designated airplane crashed before landing. Thank God my husband was able to hear and follow the angel's instruction. Thank God our friend trusted my husband enough to obey the message. Her life was spared because of her obedience to the warning. The angel of the Lord delivered our friend from an airplane crash.

Flat Tire Delay

It was one typical hot summer and my husband had worked all day. While headed back to the shop, an angel told my husband to pull over and get out of the heavy traffic. "Pull over, Preacher. Your tire is going to blow," the angel said. At the time of the warning, everything was fine. Then the angel said again, "Pull over, Preacher!" Just as soon as he found a safe place and pulled over, the tire exploded. The Lord delivered my husband from a potential accident during heavy traffic hours. Thank God for the angel that rescued my husband from danger!

Money Blessing

In 1989, my husband had an electricity bill with payment due by 4 p.m. to avoid disconnection that same day. With no available resources to pay the bill, he went to work anticipating the disconnection of his electrical services. At this time he was working from a herbicide truck spraying weed control chemical near Interstate 20.

As one of my husband's co-workers drove to their next scheduled assignment, an angel spoke to my husband and told him to keep his eyes on the grass at the right side of the highway. So he obeyed the angel's voice and looked intently at the grass for about four or five miles. Then suddenly, he saw something that looked like money scattered on the green grass. He asked his co-worker to stop the truck. When he stopped, my husband jumped out of the truck and ran back to the place where he thought he had seen the money. Sure enough, there was a lot of money on the ground! He picked up money and put it in his pockets while he yelled to his co-worker to come and pick up some money. His co-worker just sat there, apparently in disbelief. My husband ran to the truck and opened the passenger door to tell his co-worker about the money. My husband's co-worker said, "Are you sure?" My husband showed him money and told him again that there was money all over the ground. Yes, the co-worker then joined him to pick up money—not trash.

By this time, my husband knew that his utility bill would be paid before 4p.m. that day. He gave some money to another co-worker, gave some money to me, and kept the surplus money for himself. It was a large sum of money and he still remembers the word of the angel to "*keep looking to the right on the grass.*" This reminds me when Jesus told Peter to catch a fish and get money out of the fish's mouth. It pays to obey, even when it sounds like nonsense.

> *But so that we may not cause offense, go to the lake and throw out your line. Take the first fish you catch; open its mouth and you will find a four-drachma coin. Take it and give it to them for my tax and yours* (Matthew 17:27).

Car Accident Premonition

One Friday night during church services, my husband heard an angel of the Lord say: "*Tell that lady her husband is going to be involved in a vehicle accident tonight, but he will not be injured. He will not get a scratch.*" So my husband identified the lady and told her the exact words the angel had spoken to him. The lady looked at him as if he was crazy. The next day, that Saturday, one of the church members told us that the lady's husband was involved in an accident that Friday night just as my husband had forewarned her. The lady's husband was not hurt—there was not even a scratch on him, just as the angel had warned.

The following angelic encounters were shared by Evelyn Murray Drayton (a friend and sister in Christ):

Where Did That Snake Come From

When Evelyn was a young girl, one of her chores was to help keep the yard swept. Her family did not own a lawn mower; therefore, her grandfather did not allow grass to grow in his yard. Her grandfather kept yard brooms on hand that he called *flannel bushes*. Evelyn had seen her grandfather gather the flannel bushes many times and knew how to gather the wild plant.

One day Evelyn was told to sweep the yard; so, she went into the woods alone to cut her flannel bushes. While trying to gather her bushes, she noticed a multi-colored snake slithering near her foot. If she had run through the woods, there was always potential for a more dangerous outcome. She did not know about listening to the voice of angels or to the voice of the Lord; yet, in her mind, she felt an urge to stand still. Evelyn stood still even though she felt like running. She squeezed her eyes tightly as she felt the belly of the snake slithered over her foot and kept moving.

Based on her description, the snake was later identified as a non-poisonous scarlet snake. She said she told her family about the experience; but no one really believed her because they figured she would have run from the snake. As she matured and looked back over her life, Evelyn believes that an angel was there helping her to get back home safely—with her flannel bushes in hand, of course.

Construction Site Disaster

Evelyn recounted driving to the eventful city of Columbia, South Carolina. She was young, vibrant, and happy that she had recently obtained her driver's license. This accomplishment made her proud to chauffeur several family members around the city before their scheduled appointment.

As she drove in one particular area, it appeared construction work was in progress, but there were no warning signs that she recollected; so she continued her shortcut. If there were any warning signs, someone had strategically displaced them. To her surprise, she came to a dead end street with a huge construction opening in the road and the car nearly fell in the hole. She said it was only by the grace of God that her car stopped, not feet, but only inches away from the edge. She could only backup because there was no turn around space. She said she did not fully realize the extreme danger until she backed up to find a safe place to stop and calm down. She believed angels were on assignment to help and that only divine intervention saved her family that day.

Spinning Uncontrollably

Evelyn's angelic encounter occurred early one morning in 1989 on her way to work. Her commute to work was over 60 miles one way so she would leave home early in the mornings and return home late in the evenings. On this morning, just a few miles from home, a dark-colored disabled truck was parked in the middle of the road without lights.

When Evelyn realized the vehicle was around the bend in her lane, she could only apply brakes and swerve to avoid hitting the vehicle. There were ditches on both sides of the highway—what could she possibly do? Well, when Evelyn applied brakes and swerved, her car went into an uncontrollable spin. Thank God there was no oncoming traffic on this busy highway at the time.

Evelyn said she saw the ditches and prayed loudly, "Lord, please let my husband find me before I die in this ditch." As the car continued spinning and was headed for the ditch on the opposite side of the highway, something divine happened. Evelyn said she felt the car automatically controlled by another driver. Her car, literally, lifted from the highway while spinning, and then lowered back in the direction she was originally headed.

Evelyn said that angelic spin was the smoothest ride she ever had in her life. She landed so safely, it was almost as if nothing ever happened; except that her legs were shaking uncontrollably, her heart was beating faster, her eyes were filled with tears, and her mouth was filled with praise. She said she could hardly contain herself as she completed her commute to work.

Many days thereafter on her commute to work, she remembered that angelic encounter and smiled. She knew that God had dispatched angels for her life that day. Divine intervention has been a part of her life through the years— knowing Evelyn personally, I know the hand of God is upon her life.

> *"For he will command his angels concerning you*
> *to guard you in all your ways"* (Psalm 91:11).

I hope these few testimonies that I shared will encourage you to be more attentive to angelic intervention in your own life. We may not have the same experiences in life, but all of us will experience angelic support at one time or another. I believe all of us under close examination, whether or not religious, can recognize that certain unusual activities have transpired during dark moments in our lives. You may attribute your intervention to someone else or something else—but me—I know it was an angel.

Chapter Five

Frequently Asked Questions about Angels

There are many discussions about angels and whether they truly exist. Below I have provided a list of some frequently asked questions along with responses I believe will be helpful to describe angels and their existence.

1. What are angels?
Angels are ministering spirits sent forth [by God] to minister for them who shall be heirs of salvation. They are given their orders by God. Man is a little lower than angels. (Hebrews 1:14; 2:7)

2. When did God create angels?
Angels are light and Satan even tries to disguise himself as an angel of light. Could it be when God said, *"Let there be light"* angels were created at His command. Yet, the Bible does not give an exact timeframe for when God created angels. You will read various sources with all varied opinions about this question.

3. Are angels male or female?
Angels have appeared in different forms, including a fiery burning bush that was not consumed in Exodus 3:2. Based on that Scripture, one can deduce that angels are neither male nor female. Other descriptions in the Bible had angels appearing as men. Take

the story of Abraham for example. Three angels appeared before him and told him that he would bear a son with Sarah (Genesis 18:1-4). In this example, the angels appeared as masculine. Also, angels appeared in the form of men when Jesus rose from the dead (Luke 24:4). However, the names Michael and Gabriel, for example, appear to take on a masculine form.

4. Do angels have wings?

This question is often met with confused looks because throughout history, angels have been depicted in paintings and statutes as winged beings with long flowing robes and a halo over their heads. While there is some support for angels having wings within the Bible (Revelation 4:8; Isaiah 6:2), there is no implicit evidence that suggests all angels have wings. Ezekiel Chapter 10, verse 8, indicates that cherubim have wings (and hands like humans). In Jacob's dream of the ladder reaching into heaven, he described angels as ascending and descending from heaven to earth and back on a ladder (Genesis 28:10-13). This Scripture can be used as evidence to suggest that not all angels have wings. If so, would they need a ladder to ascend into the heaven?

5. Do we have guardian angels?

The Bible does not emphatically answer the question of whether we have individually assigned angels to guard us. Instead, information is provided about angels protecting us (Daniel 6:20-23; 2 Kings 6:13-17), providing us with God's word and direction (Acts 7:52-53; Luke 1:11-20), guiding our decisions (Matthew 1:20-21; Acts 8:26), and supplying our needs (Genesis 21:17- 20; 1 Kings 19:5-7). In the Old Testament, the nation of Israel was assigned the archangel Michael to protect its people (Daniel 12:1), but his job was to protect the nation of people and not individuals. The belief in guardian angels has been around for a long time; however, I found no explicit scriptural basis for having guardian angels.

6. Are angels visible or invisible?

Angels are described by the Bible as both visible and invisible. In the book of 2 Kings 6:17, Elijah was able to show his servant horses and chariots of fire that the servant could not otherwise see until God opened the servant's eyes. To many, angels were visible creatures bathed in white light. In some of the other accounts, angels were described as a presence. For example, in the story of Daniel in the lion's den, Daniel described feeling a presence but not actually seeing the angel. As long as the angel accomplishes God's purpose, we need not try to dictate which form they appear.

7. Do Christians have the authority to command angels?

Neither Christians nor any man have the authority to command angels. I found no Scriptures from the Bible containing any accounts of man being able to command angels to do our bidding. In fact, consider the story of Job. Satan tried numerous times to assert his control over the fate of Job and God's response was to allow Satan to do as he pleased as long as he did not attempt to take Job's life. From this story, we can assume that even Satan cannot defy the will of God and only God can command His angels. Many in ministry argue that when we speak God's word in Jesus name, angels respond to the words we speak when they line up with God's words.

8. Do angels marry and procreate?

Angels do not marry and they do not procreate. We know from Scripture that angels were created by God to carry out His will on earth. Matthew 22:30 supports the notion that angels do not marry and procreate. The Scripture reads, *"At the resurrection people will neither marry nor be given in marriage; they will be like the angels in heaven."*

9. Are angels to be worshipped?

Angels are not beings to be worshipped. In fact, we are taught that God is the only one that should be worshipped. Psalm 148:2 talks about angels taking pleasure in praising God. Also, consider the account of John the apostle where he falls down to worship the angel and he is told not to worship the angel. Revelation 22:9 reports what the angel said, *"I am a fellow servant with you and with your fellow prophets and with all who keep the words of this scroll. Worship God!"*

10. Can angels be counted?

The way angels are described in Scripture suggests that the numbers are too big for angels to truly be counted. Hebrews 12:22 KJV says, *"An innumerable company of angels."* In Daniel 7:10, Daniel described what he saw when the doors to heaven were opened. He said, *"Thousand thousands ministered unto him, and ten thousand times ten thousand stood before him."* Revelation 5:11 mentions *"ten thousand times ten thousand, and thousands of thousands"* of voices round about God's throne.

11. What are some Scriptures that can persuade me to believe that angels do exist?

- *Are not all **angels** ministering spirits sent to serve those who will inherit salvation?* Hebrews 1:14
- The **angel** of the LORD encamps around those who fear him, and he delivers them. Psalm 34:7
- *Do you think I cannot call on my Father, and he will at once put at my disposal more than twelve legions of **angels**?* Matthew 26:53
- *And saw two **angels** in white, seated where Jesus' body had been, one at the head and the other at the foot.* John 20:12
- *The angel said to me, "These words are trustworthy and true. The Lord, the God who inspires the prophets, sent*

his **angel** *to show his servants the things that must soon take place.* Revelation 22:6

- *This is how it will be at the end of the age. The **angels** will come and separate the wicked from the righteous.* Matthew 13:49
- *Praise the LORD, you his **angels**, you mighty ones who do his bidding, who obey his word.* Psalm 103:20
- *Human beings ate the bread of **angels**; he sent them all the food they could eat.* Psalm 78:25
- *See that you do not despise one of these little ones. For I tell you that their **angels** in heaven always see the face of my Father in heaven.* Matthew 18:10
- *And they can no longer die; for they are like the **angels**. They are God's children, since they are children of the resurrection.* Luke 20:36
- *Yet even **angels**, although they are stronger and more powerful, do not heap abuse on such beings when bringing judgment on them from the Lord.* 2 Peter 2:11
- *Do not let anyone who delights in false humility and the worship of **angels** disqualify you. Such people also go into great detail about what they have seen, and their unspiritual minds puff them up with idle notions.* Colossians 2:18
- *When the **angels** had left them and gone into heaven, the shepherds said to one another, "Let's go to Bethlehem and see this thing that has happened, which the Lord has told us about."* Luke 2:15
- *In speaking of the **angels** he says, "He makes his **angels** spirits, and his servants flames of fire."* Hebrews 1:7
- *But about that day or hour no one knows, not even the **angels** in heaven, nor the Son, but only the Father.* Matthew 24:36

Epilogue

We are to worship and pray to God only, not to angels. I like the fact that God has allowed me the joy of experiencing angelic visitation and intervention. I *know* angels do exist and will forever be of service to mankind.

Do Angels Really Exist? highlights and acknowledges the debate over whether angels really exist. I have provided various Scriptures to shed light on this debate. The answer to this question or the truth lies in our personal religious beliefs and whether or not our faith is strong enough to believe in the essence of something we are unable to see. Likewise, while many have debated the topic of an all powerful God, and His creations, it is a personal choice to acknowledge and accept Him into our hearts.

There is a lot of contradictory information in the mainstream about angels and we will probably never learn all there is to know about angels. If you chose to believe, the evidence presented throughout the Bible is irrefutable. The Bible tells us of God's purpose for angels in our lives. Angels are messengers for God, used to carry out His will. They were created to act as a channel to deliver God's purpose and direction to man, as well as to act as protectors in times of need. The story of Daniel in the lion's den and the deliverance of Lot both serve to show how God sent His angels to protect us from harm. The Bible also tells us that angels provide God with constant worship and praise. They surround His throne and guard His sacred grounds (i.e. the Garden of Eden).

We know that angels exist and we mentioned seraphim, cherubim, and thrones. Angels have been sent by God to warn of impending danger and to bring tidings of joy, as was the case with Mary and Joseph. The shepherds were visited by an angel who announced the birth of Jesus Christ. Shortly after, Joseph was warned that King Herod was looking to kill baby Jesus and that he needed to flee. Finally, we know that angels will be essential during the end of days. The list of angel encounters throughout the Bible is endless.

The belief of angels is prevalent in more than just Christian/ Protestant religions and those other religions normally describe angels with characteristics and purposes similar to those presented within the Bible.

We have enough biblical references to deter us from worshipping angels. God alone is to be worshipped by angels and by man. Man is not to place their faith in angels, but anchor their faith in God alone through Christ Jesus.

When the accounts in the Bible are coupled with the personal reports throughout history of people encountering angels in times of extreme despair and need; how can there be an argument? In addition, how can we believe in God and in Jesus Christ, but not believe in angels?

Do Angels Really Exist? May the Lord bless you and keep you in all your ways. May He continue to dispatch angels when you need them in your life. Maybe, one day you will write to me and tell me, "I saw an angel!"

Encouragement
(Paraphrased from Psalm 91)

You, my friends, are the ones who dwell in the shelter of the
Most High
and you will rest in the shadow of the Almighty.
We can say of the LORD, "He is our refuge and our fortress,
our God, in whom we trust."
Surely God will save us
from the devil's traps
and from his deadly tactics.
God will cover us with His feathers,
and under His wings we will find refuge;
God's faithfulness will be our shield and rampart.
We will not fear the terror of night,
nor the arrow that flies by day,
nor the pestilence that stalks in the darkness,
nor the plague that destroys at midday.
A thousand may fall at our side,
ten thousand at our right hand,
but it will not come near us.
We will only observe with our eyes
and see the punishment of the wicked.
If we say, "The LORD is our refuge,"
and we make the Most High our dwelling,
no harm will overtake us,
no disaster will come near our house.
For God will command His **angels** concerning us
to guard us in all our ways;
the **angels** will lift us in their hands,
so that we will not strike our foot against a stone.
We will tread on the lion and the cobra;
we will trample the great lion and the serpent.
Because I love my people," says the LORD, "I will rescue them;

I will protect them, for they acknowledge the name of the Lord
their God.
They will call on me, and I will answer them;
I will be with them in trouble,
I will deliver them and honor them.
With long life I will satisfy my people,
and show them my salvation.

Special Notes

Special Notes

Special Notes

Special Notes

About the Author

Dr. Sandra Carter Snyder, formerly of Atlanta, Georgia, and affectionately known as Sandie, is an ordained evangelist and phenomenal speaker, who inspires, motivates, encourages, and influences people with positive result to reach their full potential and to be like Christ Jesus. She enjoys lecturing on angelic encounters.

Sandie has earned Bachelor, Master, and Doctorate degrees in divinity and graduated magna cum laude. She is a Board certified Christian counselor and therapist, Board certified pastoral counselor, certified grief counselor, certified temperament counselor, certified life skill coach, and anger practitioner. She has also completed Angel Love Practitioner Training in Atlanta, Georgia.

Sandie is a member of Georgia Christian Counselors Association, Restoration Theology Seminary (RTS) Alumni Association, Individual Crisis Intervention, and Women Business Association. Sandie also served as an outreach counselor with the world renowned Billy Graham Evangelistic crusades in Atlanta, Georgia. She loves to travel and has made mission trips to Honduras and other countries.

Sandie has phenomenal entrepreneurial skills. She is founder and CEO of Inview Outreach Ministries Inc., which empowers those in need and offers a choice to change for a lifetime by providing spiritual, social, economic, emotional and physical resource support. She is also owner of Inview Upscale Consignment Shop and owner of Empowerment Enrichment Counseling Services LLC.

Evangelist Snyder has experience in radio broadcasting and hosted her own radio show called, Inspiration Time. She has also appeared on various television panels. Sandie is proud to publish her first book titled, Do Angels Really Exist?

Sandie would appreciate your questions and/or comments. Email her at inviewaskme@yahoo.com.

You may also contact her at the following mailing address:
Sandra C. Snyder
1933 South Fraser Street
Georgetown, SC 29440

Telephone: 843-494-2575